About Cyber Reads:

Unleashing the Power of Books in the Digital Age,
In an era dominated by digital technologies and virtual experiences,
the publishing industry has witnessed a significant transformation.
As literature adapts to the fast-paced digital world, a new player
has emerged, revolutionizing the way books are produced,
distributed, and consumed: Cyber Reads, a visionary book
publisher at the forefront of the digital revolution. In this book, we
will delve into the innovative practices and impact of Cyber Reads,
providing dead accurate exam guidelines for your next certifications
in Digital and Security based certifications.

Question Set 1

QUESTION 1

You configure a cloud-based printer in Dynamics 365 Business Central.

Purchase orders printed by users must automatically print to the cloud-based

printer. You need to create a setup record for the user, report, and printer

combination.

On which page should you create the setup record?

A. Printer Selections
B. Printer Management
C. Report Layout Selection
D. Report Selection – Purchase
E. Document Sending Profiles

QUESTION 2

You are implementing Dynamics 365 BusinessCentral Online.

Users must be added to Business Central for the first time. You need to add the

users.

Which action should you use?

A. Get New Users from Office 365
B. Create a new entry on the User Setup page
C. Update Users from Office 365
D. Import User Groups

QUESTION 3
DRAG DROP

You set up a new company for a customer.

The customer provides you with a Microsoft Excel file that contains master data.

You need to import the master data by using configuration packages.

Which four actions should you perform in sequence? To answer, move the appropriate actions from the list of actions to the answer area and arrange them in the correct order.

Select and Place:

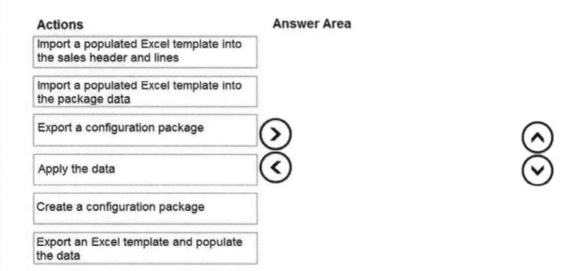

Actions

Import a populated Excel template into the sales header and lines

Import a populated Excel template into the package data

Export a configuration package

Apply the data

Create a configuration package

Export an Excel template and populate the data

Answer Area

QUESTION 4
DRAG DROP

You are setting up approval workflows in Dynamics 365 Business Central. You

need to configure approval limits.

Which approver limit types should you use? To answer, drag the appropriate
approver limit types to the correct requirements. Each approver limit type may
be used once, or not at all. You may need to drag the split bar between panes
or scroll to view content.

NOTE: Each correct selection is worth one point.

Select and Place:

Approver limit types		Answer Area	
Direct approver		**Requirement**	**Approver limit type**
Specific approver		Route approval requests to the approver defined in Approval User Setup, regardless of the amount.	Approver limit type
First Qualified approver		Route approval requests to the approver defined in the Workflow Response, regardless of the amount.	Approver limit type
Approver Chain		Route approval requests to a user who can approve requests for the required amount.	Approver limit type

QUESTION 5

A company uses Dynamics 365 Business Central.

The company wants to print financial statements by using a cloud-based printer.

You need to recommend the type of printer the customer should install.

Which type of printer should you recommend?

A. Email
B. System
C. Client default
D. Server default

QUESTION 6

You create a test instance of Dynamics 365 Business Central and enter

transactions for testing purposes. You create a production company instance in

the same Business Central environment. You need to copy the setup and

master data from the test instance to the production instance without copying

transaction data.

What are two possible ways to achieve the goal? Each correct answer presents
a complete solution.

NOTE: Each correct selection is worth one point.

A. Use the Run Migration Now function from Cloud Migration Management
B. Create and export a configuration package from the source company. Next,
   import into the destination company
C. Use the Copy Data from Company function from the Configuration
   Worksheet page
D. Use the Copy function from the Companies page

QUESTION 7

DRAG DROP

You are creating companies for multiple customers in the cloud-based version

of Dynamics 365 Business Central by using the assisted setup guide. You need

to create new companies.

Which templates should you use? To answer, drag the appropriate templates to
the correct requirements. Each template may be used once, more than once, or
not at all. You may need to drag the split bar between panes or scroll to view
content.

NOTE: Each correct selection is worth one point.

Select and Place:

Templates		Answer Area	
		Requirement	**Template**
Create New		Create a company that has setup data and sample data.	Template
Evaluation		Create a company that does not have setup data.	Template
Production		Create a blank company that has setup data but does not have sample data.	Template

Testlet 2

This is a case study. **Case studies are not timed separately. You can use as much exam time as you would like to complete each case**. However, there may be additional case studies and sections on this exam. You must manage your time to ensure that you are able to complete all questions included on this exam in the time provided.

To answer the questions included in a case study, you will need to reference information that is provided in the case study. Case studies might contain exhibits and other resources that provide more information about the scenario that isdescribed in the case study. Each question is independent of the other questions in this case study.

At the end of this case study, a review screen will appear. This screen allows you to review your answers and to make changes before you move to the next section of the exam. After you begin a new section, you cannot return to this section.

To start the case study

To display the first question in the case study, click the **Next** button. Use the buttons in the left pane to explore the content of the case study before you answer the questions. Clicking these buttons displays information such as businessrequirements, existing environment, and problem statements. When you are ready to answer a question, click the **Question** button to return to the question. **Current environment**

Cash and carry sales

- When a customer makes a purchase at the company's cash and carry desk, the sale is handwritten on a three-part form.
- The cash and carry associate retrieves the items listed on the order from the warehouse.
- Special prices and discounts are used to move products that will expire soon or that are overstocked.
- Cash is accepted for payments.
- The cash drawer is balanced at the end of every day. A deposit is created for the cash and given to the accountant.

Brokered sales orders

Brokered sales are called in to customer service by the brokers and sometimes directly by customers. The sales are entered into QuickBooks. Becauseinventory is not tracked in QuickBooks, the generic item **Brokered Item** is used.

- Two copies of the packing slip and printed from QuickBooks and sent to the warehouse.

Order picking

- The warehouse manager provides a container and the two copies of the
- packing slip to a picker.Items that are out of stock are marked on both copies of the packing slip.
- The shipping amount is determined and written on the packing slips.
- One copy of the completed packing slip is placed in a basket for customer service. Completed orders are boxed up with a copy of the invoice and shipped to customers.

Order invoicing

- Throughout the day, the customer service manager collects the packing slip copies and updates the invoices in QuickBooks.
- The customer service manager adds a line for shipping with the amount provided by the packer.
- The customer service manager prints a copy of the final invoice and sends it to the warehouse.
- The accountant uses Microsoft Word to create weekly invoices for all shipments invoiced in QuickBooks during the week for some customers.

Cash and carry sales

One-line sales invoices are saved in QuickBooks for each cash and carry sale to a miscellaneous customer.Customer details for cash and carry sales are not kept in QuickBooks. **Deposits**

The accountant receives the deposit bag from the cash and carry sales desk at the end of every day. Receipts are recorded in QuickBooks against cash and carry and brokered sales based on the deposit slips.

Brokers commission

Brokers fees are paid as a percentage of sales.
A Sales by Product/Service Summary report is run in QuickBooks every month for Brokered Item to calculate what is owned.

RequirementsCustomers

Users with permission must be able to quickly add new customers.
The original source of all customers in the accounting system must be identified to be from cash and carry or brokered sales.The company needs to keep a record of special price promotions given to specific customers.
Customers must be identified with a unique general business posting group

so that the correct freight G/L account is used in sales transactions.

Sales

The customer source must be used to identify the business line, and the customer source must be indicated on every sales transactions. Customer service and cash and carry desk associates must be able to enter sales into Dynamics 365 Business Central by customer.

If a customer is not already listed in the system, a cash and carry associate or customer service associate must be able to quickly add the new customer in the process of recording the first sale.A point-of-sale system is not needed, but users must be able to record which items are purchased by customers, accept and record their payment, and print receipts indicating paid in full.

Items

The sales manager and warehouse manager must be able to set a specific timeframe for special promotion discounts on items.For special promotions, discounts must be consistent for all items in a product line using a single discount calculation.

Special pricing may be given to a retail chain or buying group. This pricing must be automatically applied when an order is taken for any of these customers. The original price must be recorded with each sale.

Customers must always be charged the lowest amount for an item at the time of the sale. For example, an overstocked olive oil has a regular price of $20 per unit. Customers in a buying group for restaurants can buy it for $18 per unit.

There is an autumn promotion price for the item at $19 per unit. However, on a specific day only, there is an overstock special at a 15 percent discount off the regular price. **Sales invoices**

Warehouse workers must be able to indicate the following in the system for each order:
1. the items picked
2. the shipping charges
3. notifications, if any, that customer service needs to provide to the customer

Items sold at a discount must show the original price, discount, and net amount on each line of the invoice. Invoices must be posted at the cash and carry desk at the time of sale. For orders, accounting must post invoices and send them tocustomers.

Warehouse employees must be able to indicate what has been shipped on an order. They will use the G/L account for shipping charges. They need to use the correct G/L account for sales versus cost through proper assignment of salesand purchase accounts in the general posting setup.

Some of the brokered customers require one invoice per week regardless of the number of orders or shipments. **Accounts**

Payment terms vary by customer.

The amount paid to brokers must be calculated from sales after invoice discounts.Broker vendors must be easily identifiable from other vendors in lists

Commission paid on sales not collected within 120 days must be deducted from brokers' next compensation payment.

Reporting

Wide World Importers requires reporting on the following:

the overall profitability of each line of business at any time for any given period

the cost of outbound shipping in the overall profitability of sales by business line in all related reportsfreight sales and cost by account in the trial balance

the cost of brokers' compensation in reporting the overall profitability of sales by business linethe effect of item discount promotions in financial statements.

Issues Pricing

Spreadsheets are used to maintain special item pricing and discounts. The only source of product line discount information is a whiteboard in the warehouse. The price charged is frequently incorrect.

Customers complain when they think they think they have not received the best price available. Promotions are sometimes applied in error after a special pricing event ends, for example, when discounts are offered temporarily to reduceoverstock.

Management cannot see original versus actual price on all sales. Discounts given by brokers requires spreadsheets and comparison between price list and price on sales invoice. Management needs to be able to quickly see the discountgiven on each sale.

Payment terms

Agreed-upon payment terms are frequently entered incorrectly on orders, causing cashflow issues.

Invoices already paid in full exist on the sales aging reports. The frequent cause of this issue is that sales from the cash and carry desk are not indicated as cash sales and are not posted as paid in full. Some buying groups require that all invoices sent during a month be due on the 20th of the following month.

Invoicing

Paperwork is frequently misplaced between the warehouse, customer service, and accounting.

Invoices that are posted in the accounting system based on shipments and invoices that are sent to customers weekly do not match due to errors transferring the data from one document to another.Users are selecting the incorrect freight type (expense versus sales) on purchase and sales transactions, making it difficult to reconcile freight costs.

Sales placed from the cash and carry desk by customers originally acquired through a broker are not being recognized with the correct customer source. Reporting by business line is inaccurate.

Accounts

Users often forget which fields to use to enter information when they add new customers to QuickBooks. This results in errors and inconsistencies in data and affects sales reporting. Confidence in sales reporting accuracy is low. Adding new brokers is a different process than adding other purchase vendors. Users often forget which fields to select and how to correctly assign the vendor number to add new brokers.

QUESTION 1

HOTSPOT

You need to report profitability by business line.

How should you configure the system? To answer, select the appropriate options in the answer area.

NOTE: Each correct selection is worth one point.

Hot Area:

Answer Area

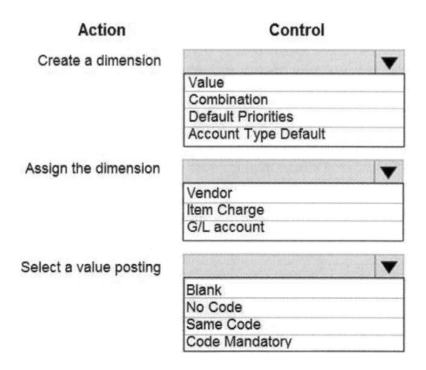

Action	Control
Create a dimension	Value / Combination / Default Priorities / Account Type Default
Assign the dimension	Vendor / Item Charge / G/L account
Select a value posting	Blank / No Code / Same Code / Code Mandatory

Testlet 3

This is a case study. **Case studies are not timed separately. You can use as much exam time as you would like to complete each case**. However, there may be additional case studies and sections on this exam. You must manage your time to ensure that you are able to complete all questions included on this exam in the time provided.

To answer the questions included in a case study, you will need to reference information that is provided in the case study. Case studies might contain exhibits and other resources that provide more information about the scenario that isdescribed in the case study. Each question is independent of the other questions in this case study.

At the end of this case study, a review screen will appear. This screen allows you to review your answers and to make changes before you move to the next section of the exam. After you begin a new section, you cannot return to this section.

To start the case study

To display the first question in the case study, click the **Next** button. Use the buttons in the left pane to explore the content of the case study before you answer the questions. Clicking these buttons displays information such as businessrequirements, existing environment, and problem statements. When you are ready to answer a question, click the **Question** button to return to the question. **Current environment**

Deliveries

   The company receives daily truckloads of products from their vendors, warehouses the products briefly, and then ships orders based on a weekly delivery cycle to each customer's store.Customers have regular standing orders that are revised and finished one week prior to delivery.
   Best for You Organics has a fleet of trucks that make deliveries according to planned routes.
   The company also has a floating route for trucks to deliver rush orders. The route is being used more often by customers and has overwhelmed the warehouse with exception processing.

Duties

The company wants to provide greater separation of duties between activities in the office and activities in the warehouse.

The accounting team enters orders for the sales team, sends pick tickers back to the warehouse, and organizes shipping documents. The accounting team invoices the orders when they receive instructions from the warehouse that an order shipped.

Employees have expressed frustration because they need to work longer hours to accommodate the increase in sales.The company does not use the Advanced Warehousing function.

RequirementsSalespeople

Salespeople must be able to manage opportunities that are converted to quotes.
Salespeople must be able to release orders to the warehouse to be fulfilled once a quote is final.
Salespeople must be trained on how to determine if inventory is available

when they are completing the quote to avoid promising inventory that is not on hand because all orders are processed one week in advance of delivery. **Team**

responsibilities

Deliveries must be shipped daily by employees in the warehouse. The office must be responsible for completing the invoicing process.The current team responsibilities are shown in the following graphic:

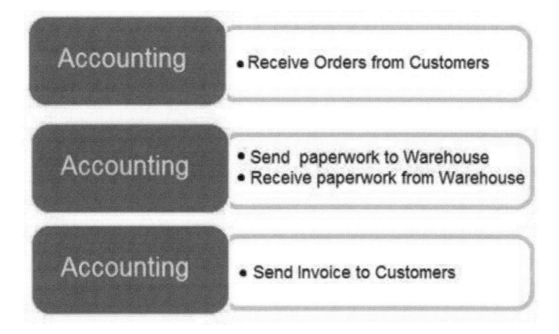

The required team responsibilities are shown in the following graphic:

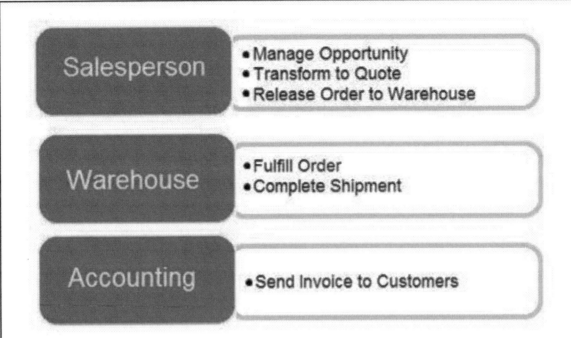

Vendor management

The company contracts with each vendor for regular discounts at the invoice level.

The company requires a pre-set discount percentage to calculate automatically when the purchaser completes a purchase order.

The company must be able to see a copy of the completed purchase order in

the system when they have new contract negotiations with their vendors.

Customerand inventory management

Sales invoices must be automatically emailed by the system to customers. A template must be used for emails sent to customers. The template must not be-altered.Customers who pre-pay their invoices must not receive a copy of their invoices.

The company warehouses all products as Case quantities. The company has difficulty recording accurate costs for product returns. The company wants to expand their capabilities for managing returns by setting up all inventory in a quantity of Each.

Reporting

The company must be able to answer two key questions when they report financial results:

Which customers are buying which items? Which salespeople are selling in which regions?

When discussing customers, the company must refer to each Customer Group as follows:

- Big Box Franchise
- Private

When discussing items, the company must refer to each Item Group as follows:

- Fair Trade Free RangeGrass Fed Heirloom Organic

Salesperson names that must be used are:

- SalespersonASalespersonBSalespersonCSalespersonD

Region names that must be used are:

- NorthSouthEast West

Commission

The company must be able to track salesperson performance within certain regions to calculate commission.Each salesperson must be assigned only to a single region.

This commission data is currently recorded inconsistently, resulting in incorrect combinations that require manual correction. The company must have some level of automation to manage this.

Issues Issue 1

The accounting team needs an improved process for reconciling inventory to the general ledger.

Posted transactions are changing financial reporting in periods that have been closed. Unexpected changes in inventory cost for previous months are causing costing inaccuracies.The system must restrict the adjustment of costs for closed months.

The new policy will be to restrict all users to posting in the current month only, with the exception of a few employees from the accounting teamThe calendar fiscal year for company must begin on June 1.

Issue 2

The accounting team uses a complex manual accrual process to determine the accounting impact of items received but not invoiced. The system must streamline the item accrual process.

Issue 3

The company often receives a higher quantity of produce items than what they order because vendors allow for spoilage or damage of produce in transit. The company does not want to allow over receipt on non-produce items.

Issue 4

The company has received comments from their auditors that invoices are not being properly compared to received inventory documents before they are posted. The company does not use warehouse management and always handlesprocesses directly from the purchase order. The company always has the following documents:

Purchase order from the procurement department receiving document from the warehouse   electronicinvoice from the vendor

QUESTION 1
HOTSPOT

You need to configure reporting.

What should you do? To answer, select the appropriate options in the answer area.

NOTE: Each correct selection is worth one point.

Hot Area:

Answer Area

Requirement	Action
Set up dimensions	▼
	Create a new entry on Dimensions
	Select a dimension on Sales & Receivables Setup
	Choose a code in the Dimensions FastTab on General Ledger Setup
	Add default dimensions to General Ledger Accounts
Configure global dimensions	▼
	Change global dimensions on General Ledger Setup
	Add a global dimension on General Ledger Setup
	Assign a dimension value of Global to Dimensions
	Select Global Dimensions on all Setup pages
Configure shortcut dimensions	▼
	Choose a shortcut dimension code on General Ledger Setup
	Assign a dimension value of Shortcut to Dimensions
	Add default dimensions to Master Records
	Choose dimensions on an Analysis View

Question Set 1

QUESTION 1

You are creating payment terms.

A company processes standard vendor payments on the seventh day of the

next month. You need to set up payment terms for the vendor.

Which date formula should you use?

A. 37D
B. 1M+7D
C. 1M+6D
D. CM+7D

QUESTION 2

A company purchases items by using cash. You register a vendor payment

when you a post a purchase invoice for a cash vendor. You are creating a new

cash vendor.

You need to set up the vendor so that payments post automatically when you

post a purchase invoice. Which type of setup should you use?

A. Payment Method as Cash
B. Payment Term as COD
C. Payment Method as Cash with balancing account
D. Prepayment

QUESTION 3
DRAG DROP

You need to configure a new journal template.

What should you do? To answer, drag the appropriate fields to the correct requirements. Each field may be used once, more than once, or not at all. You may need to drag the split bar between panes or scroll to view content.

NOTE: Each correct selection is worth one point.

Select and Place:

Fields

Force Doc. Balance

Bal. Account Type and Bal. Account No.

Source Code

Reason Code

Answer Area

Requirement	Field
Create journal lines that must balance by document number and document type.	Field
Create journal lines that must specify a default balancing account.	Field
Create journal lines that use the origin of the entry as the basis for an audit trail.	Field
Create journal lines that must include a reason why an entry was made and can be used for the audit trail.	Field

QUESTION 4 Monetary amounts for local currency must always display three decimal places.

In General Ledger Setup, you need to configure the appropriate setup field with the appropriate value.

What should you do?

A. Set the value of **Amount Decimal Places** to **3:3**

B. Set the value of Unit-Amount Decimal Places to 3:3

C. Set the value of Inv. Rounding Precision to 0.001

D. Set the value of Unit-Amount Rounding Precision to 0.001

E. Set the value of Amount Rounding Precision to 0.001

QUESTION 5 HOTSPOT

A bank is implementing Dynamics 365 Business Central.

Each bank account must be configured to a unique G/L Account. You need to

set up the first bank account.

How should you configure the system? To answer, select the appropriate options in the answer area.

NOTE: Each correct selection is worth one point.

Hot Area:

Answer Area

Control	Assignment
Bank Account Nos.	▼
	Bank Account Posting groups
	General Ledger Setup
	Cash Flow Setup
	Source Code Setup
G/L Account for the bank account	▼
	General Business Posting group
	Bank Account Posting group
	General Posting Setup
	Bank Account Currency Code

QUESTION 6

A company has been using Dynamics 365 Business Central for many years.

A new accounting manager for the company reviews the chart of accounts. The manager wants to remove some general ledger accounts. The Check G/L Account Usage field is selected in the General Ledger Setup.
You need to assist with the account deletions.

What is one requirement that enables deletion of a general ledger account?

A. The account cannot be used in any posting groups or posting setup
B. The fiscal year needs to be closed
C. The general ledger account must be of the type Balance Sheet
D. The general ledger account is configured to allow for deletion

QUESTION 7

The general ledger account for accounts receivable must match the sum of all balances on the customer cards. You need to set up the general ledger account card for accounts receivable to meet this requirement.

Which configuration should you use?

A. Account Type
B. Blocked
C. Totaling
D. Direct Posting

QUESTION 8

HOTSPOT

A company uses Dynamics 365 Business Central.

The company wants to automate sales credit memo processing. You need to configure the system to meet the requirements.

What should you do? To answer, select the appropriate options in the answer area.

NOTE: Each correct selection is worth one point.

Hot Area:

Answer Area

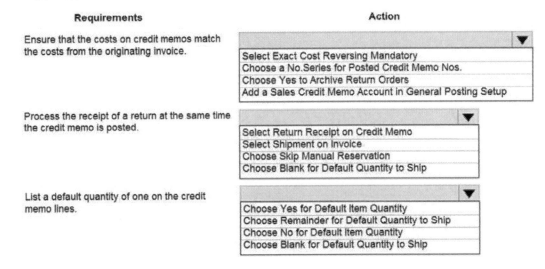

Requirements	Action
Ensure that the costs on credit memos match the costs from the originating invoice.	Select Exact Cost Reversing Mandatory Choose a No.Series for Posted Credit Memo Nos. Choose Yes to Archive Return Orders Add a Sales Credit Memo Account in General Posting Setup
Process the receipt of a return at the same time the credit memo is posted.	Select Return Receipt on Credit Memo Select Shipment on Invoice Choose Skip Manual Reservation Choose Blank for Default Quantity to Ship
List a default quantity of one on the credit memo lines.	Choose Yes for Default Item Quantity Choose Remainder for Default Quantity to Ship Choose No for Default Item Quantity Choose Blank for Default Quantity to Ship

QUESTION 9
DRAG DROP

You are implementing Dynamics 365 Business Central. The accounting

manager of the company provides you with the chart of accounts. You need to

set up specific posting groups according to the chart of accounts.

Which setup should you use? To answer, drag the appropriate setup to the correct action. Each setup may be used once, more than once, or not at all. You may need to drag the split bar between panes or scroll to view content.

NOTE: Each correct selection is worth one point.

Select and Place:

Setups
Bank Account Posting Groups
Customer Posting Groups
Inventory Posting Groups and Inventory Posting Setup
Vendor Posting Groups
General Posting Setup

Answer Area

Action	Setup
Automatic posting of received payment differences	Setup
Automatic posting to the payables account	Setup
Automatic posting to different work in progress balance accounts, depending on the location	Setup

QUESTION 10
An accounting manager provides you with a chart of accounts.

The accounting manager wants you to configure the General Posting Setup.

You need to complete the configuration as efficiently as possible.

What are three ways to complete the configuration? Each correct answer presents a complete solution.

NOTE: Each correct selection is worth one point.

A. Use the Copy action to create a new General Posting Setup Card
B. Import a configuration package that contains the General Posting Setup
C. Use the Suggest Accounts action to create all possible posting setup combinations
D. Create a new General Posting Setup Card, and then use the Suggest Accounts action
E. Create a new General Posting Setup Card, and then use the Copy action

QUESTION 11
HOTSPOT

A company is implementing Dynamics 365 Business Central.

The accountant must be able to report discounts received on purchased items

separately from costs.You need to configure the system to meet the

requirement.

How should you configure the system? To answer, select the appropriate
configurations in the answer area.

NOTE: Each correct selection is worth one point.

Hot Area:

Answer Area

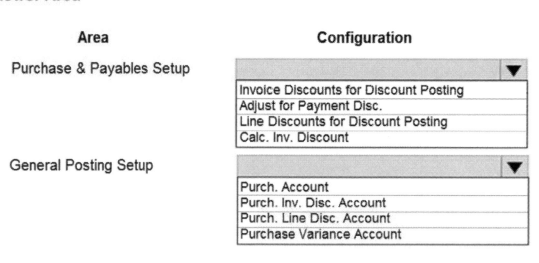

Area	Configuration
Purchase & Payables Setup	▼
	Invoice Discounts for Discount Posting
	Adjust for Payment Disc.
	Line Discounts for Discount Posting
	Calc. Inv. Discount
General Posting Setup	▼
	Purch. Account
	Purch. Inv. Disc. Account
	Purch. Line Disc. Account
	Purchase Variance Account

Testlet 2

This is a case study. **Case studies are not timed separately. You can use as much exam time as you would like to complete each case**. However, there may be additional case studies and sections on this exam. You must manage your time to ensure that you are able to complete all questions included on this exam in the time provided.

To answer the questions included in a case study, you will need to reference information that is provided in the case study. Case studies might contain exhibits and other resources that provide more information about the scenario that isdescribed in the case study. Each question is independent of the other questions in this case study.

At the end of this case study, a review screen will appear. This screen allows you to review your answers and to make changes before you move to the next section of the exam. After you begin a new section, you cannot return to this section.

To start the case study

To display the first question in the case study, click the **Next** button. Use the buttons in the left pane to explore the content of the case study before you answer the questions. Clicking these buttons displays information such as businessrequirements, existing environment, and problem statements. When you are ready to answer a question, click the **Question** button to return to the question. **Current environment**

Cash and carry sales

When a customer makes a purchase at the company's cash and carry desk, the sale is handwritten on a three-part form.The cash and carry associate retrieves the items listed on the order from the warehouse.
Special prices and discounts are used to move products that will expire soon or that are overstocked.Cash is accepted for payments.
The cash drawer is balanced at the end of every day. A deposit is created for the cash and given to the accountant.

Brokered sales orders

Brokered sales are called in to customer service by the brokers and sometimes directly by customers. The sales are entered into QuickBooks. Becauseinventory is not tracked in QuickBooks, the generic item **Brokered Item** is used.
Two copies of the packing slip and printed from QuickBooks and sent to the warehouse.

Order picking

The warehouse manager provides a container and the two copies of the packing slip to a picker.Items that are out of stock are marked on both copies of the packing slip.
The shipping amount is determined and written on the packing slips.
One copy of the completed packing slip is placed in a basket for customer service. Completed orders are boxed up with a copy of the invoice and shipped to customers.

Order invoicing

Throughout the day, the customer service manager collects the packing slip copies and updates the invoices in QuickBooks.The customer service manager adds a line for shipping with the amount provided by the packer.
The customer service manager prints a copy of the final invoice and sends it to the warehouse.
The accountant uses Microsoft Word to create weekly invoices for all shipments invoiced in QuickBooks during the week for some customers.

Cash and carry sales

One-line sales invoices are saved in QuickBooks for each cash and carry sale to a miscellaneous customer.Customer details for cash and carry sales are not kept in QuickBooks. **Deposits**

The accountant receives the deposit bag from the cash and carry sales desk at the end of every day. Receipts are recorded in QuickBooks against cash and carry and brokered sales based on the deposit slips.

Brokers commission

Brokers fees are paid as a percentage of sales.
A Sales by Product/Service Summary report is run in QuickBooks every month for Brokered Item to calculate what is owned.

RequirementsCustomers

Users with permission must be able to quickly add new customers.
The original source of all customers in the accounting system must be identified to be from cash and carry or brokered sales.The company needs to keep a record of special price promotions given to specific customers.
Customers must be identified with a unique general business posting group so that the correct freight G/L account is used in sales transactions.

Sales

The customer source must be used to identify the business line, and the customer source must be indicated on every sales transactions. Customer service and cash and carry desk associates must be able to enter sales into Dynamics 365 Business Central by customer.

If a customer is not already listed in the system, a cash and carry associate or customer service associate must be able to quickly add the new customer in the process of recording the first sale.A point-of-sale system is not needed, but users must be able to record which items are purchased by customers, accept and record their payment, and print receipts indicating paid in full.

Items

The sales manager and warehouse manager must be able to set a specific timeframe for special promotion discounts on items.For special promotions, discounts must be consistent for all items in a product line using a single discount calculation.

Customers must always be charged the lowest amount for an item at the time of the sale. For example, an overstocked olive oil has a regular price of $20 per unit. Customers in a buying group for restaurants can buy it for $18 per unit. There is an autumn promotion price for the item at $19 per unit. However, on a specific day only, there is an overstock special at a 15 percent discount off the regular price. **Sales invoices**

Warehouse workers must be able to indicate the following in the system for each order:
1. the items picked
2. the shipping charges
3. notifications, if any, that customer service needs to provide to the customer
   Items sold at a discount must show the original price, discount, and net amount on each line of the invoice. Invoices must be posted at the cash and carry desk at the time of sale. For orders, accounting must post invoices and send them tocustomers.
   Warehouse employees must be able to indicate what has been shipped on an order. They will use the G/L account for shipping charges. They need to use the correct G/L account for sales versus cost through proper assignment of salesand purchase accounts in the general posting setup.
   Some of the brokered customers require one invoice per week regardless of the number of orders or shipments. **Accounts**

Payment terms vary by customer.
The amount paid to brokers must be calculated from sales after invoice discounts.Broker vendors must be easily identifiable from other vendors in lists
Commission paid on sales not collected within 120 days must be deducted from brokers' next compensation payment.

Reporting

Wide World Importers requires reporting on the following:

the overall profitability of each line of business at any time for any given period

the cost of outbound shipping in the overall profitability of sales by business line in all related reportsfreight sales and cost by account in the trial balance

the cost of brokers' compensation in reporting the overall profitability of sales by business linethe effect of item discount promotions in financial statements.

Issues Pricing

Spreadsheets are used to maintain special item pricing and discounts. The only source of product line discount information is a whiteboard in the warehouse. The price charged is frequently incorrect.

Customers complain when they think they think they have not received the best price available. Promotions are sometimes applied in error after a special pricing event ends, for example, when discounts are offered temporarily to reduceoverstock.

Management cannot see original versus actual price on all sales. Discounts given by brokers requires spreadsheets and comparison between price list and price on sales invoice. Management needs to be able to quickly see the discountgiven on each sale.

Payment terms

Agreed-upon payment terms are frequently entered incorrectly on orders, causing cashflow issues.

Invoices already paid in full exist on the sales aging reports. The frequent cause of this issue is that sales from the cash and carry desk are not indicated as cash sales and are not posted as paid in full. Somebuying groups require that all invoices sent during a month be due on the 20th of the following month.

Invoicing

Paperwork is frequently misplaced between the warehouse, customer service, and accounting.

Invoices that are posted in the accounting system based on shipments and invoices that are sent to customers weekly do not match due to errors transferring the data from one document to another.Users are selecting the incorrect freight type (expense versus sales) on purchase and sales transactions, making it difficult to reconcile freight costs.

Sales placed from the cash and carry desk by customers originally acquired through a broker are not being recognized with the correct customer source. Reporting by business line is inaccurate.

Accounts

Users often forget which fields to use to enter information when they add new customers to QuickBooks. This results in errors and inconsistencies in data and affects sales reporting. Confidence in sales reporting accuracy is low.Adding new brokers is a different process than adding other purchase vendors. Users often forget which fields to select and how to correctly assign the vendor number to add new brokers.

QUESTION 1 You need to configure sales for the cashand carry desk.

What should you select?

A. Payment Service
B. Direct Debit Mandate with a value of **OneOff** for Type of Payment
C. Payment Method with a value of **Bank Account** for Balance Account
D. Payment Terms with a value of **0D** for Due Date Calculation

QUESTION 2

HOTSPOT

You need to configure the system to show the sales discounts.

How should you configure the system? To answer, select the appropriate options in the answer area.

NOTE: Each correct selection is worth one point.

Hot Area:

Answer Area

Quantity	Discount type parameter
10	Begin Quantity / End Quantity / Percentage
20	Begin Quantity / End Quantity / Percentage
42	Begin Quantity / End Quantity / Percentage

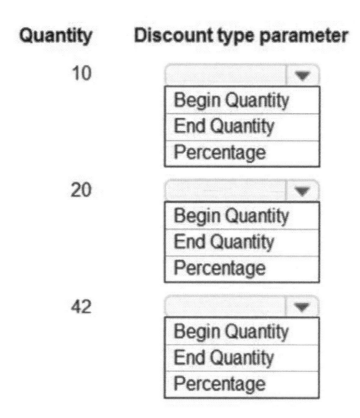

QUESTION 3
HOTSPOT

You need to resolve the reconciliation issues.

How should you complete the setup? To answer, select the appropriate options in the answer area.

NOTE: Each correct selection is worth one point.

Hot Area:

Answer Area

Configure	Control

Restrict use on

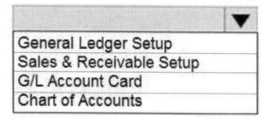

| General Ledger Setup |
| Sales & Receivable Setup |
| G/L Account Card |
| Chart of Accounts |

Set value for

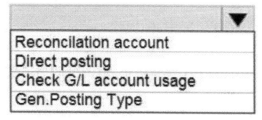

| Reconcilation account |
| Direct posting |
| Check G/L account usage |
| Gen.Posting Type |

Testlet 3

This is a case study. **Case studies are not timed separately. You can use as much exam time as you would like to complete each case**. However, there may be additional case studies and sections on this exam. You must manage your time to ensure that you are able to complete all questions included on this exam in the time provided.

To answer the questions included in a case study, you will need to reference information that is provided in the case study. Case studies might contain exhibits and other resources that provide more information about the scenario that isdescribed in the case study. Each question is independent of the other questions in this case study.

At the end of this case study, a review screen will appear. This screen allows you to review your answers and to make changes before you move to the next section of the exam. After you begin a new section, you cannot return to this section.

To start the case study

To display the first question in the case study, click the **Next** button. Use the buttons in the left pane to explore the content of the case study before you answer the questions. Clicking these buttons displays information such as businessrequirements, existing environment, and problem statements. When you are ready to answer a question, click the **Question** button to return to the question. **Current environment**

Deliveries

The company receives daily truckloads of products from their vendors, warehouses the products briefly, and then ships orders based on a weekly delivery cycle to each customer's store.Customers have regular standing orders that are revised and finished one week prior to delivery.
Best for You Organics has a fleet of trucks that make deliveries according to planned routes.
The company also has a floating route for trucks to deliver rush orders. The route is being used more often by customers and has overwhelmed the warehouse with exception processing.

Duties

The company wants to provide greater separation of duties between activities in the office and activities in the warehouse.

The accounting team enters orders for the sales team, sends pick tickers back to the warehouse, and organizes shipping documents. The accounting team invoices the orders when they receive instructions from the warehouse that an ordershipped.

Employees have expressed frustration because they need to work longer hours to accommodate the increase in sales. The company does not use the Advanced Warehousing function.

RequirementsSalespeople

Salespeople must be able to manage opportunities that are converted to quotes.
Salespeople must be able to release orders to the warehouse to be fulfilled once a quote is final.
Salespeople must be trained on how to determine if inventory is available

when they are completing the quote to avoid promising inventory that is not on hand because all orders are processed one week in advance of delivery. **Team**

responsibilities

Deliveries must be shipped daily by employees in the warehouse. The office must be responsible for completing the invoicing process. The current team responsibilities are shown in the following graphic:

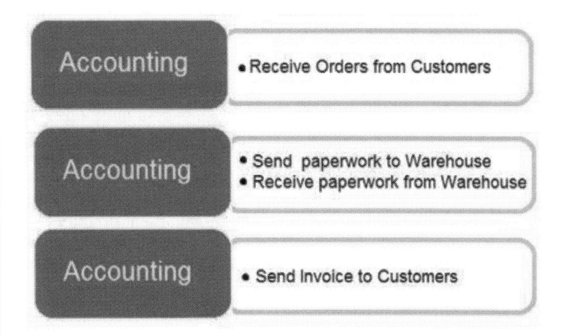

The required team responsibilities are shown in the following graphic:

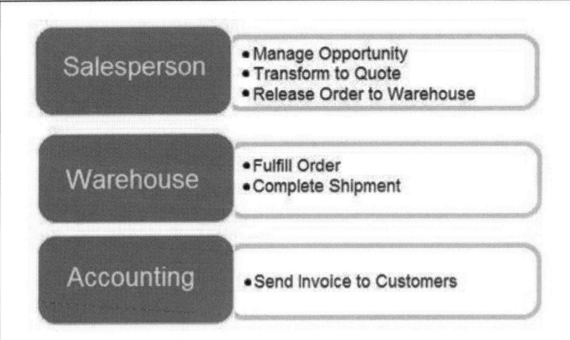

Salesperson	• Manage Opportunity • Transform to Quote • Release Order to Warehouse
Warehouse	• Fulfill Order • Complete Shipment
Accounting	• Send Invoice to Customers

Vendor management

The company contracts with each vendor for regular discounts at the invoice level.
The company requires a pre-set discount percentage to calculate automatically when the purchaser completes a purchase order.
The company must be able to see a copy of the completed purchase order in

the system when they have new contract negotiations with their vendors.

Customerand inventory management

Sales invoices must be automatically emailed by the system to customers.
A template must be used for emails sent to customers. The template must not be altered.Customers who pre-pay their invoices must not receive a copy of their invoices.
The company warehouses all products as Case quantities. The company has difficulty recording accurate costs for product returns. The company wants to expand their capabilities for managing returns by setting up all inventory in a quantity of Each.

Reporting

The company must be able to answer two key questions when they report

financial results:Which customers are buying which items?
Which salespeople are selling in which regions?

When discussing customers, the company must refer to each Customer Group

as follows:Big Box

Franchise

Private

When discussing items, the company must refer to each Item Group as follows:

Fair Trade Free RangeGrass Fed Heirloom
Organic

Salesperson names that must be used are:

SalespersonASalespersonBSalespersonCSalespersonD

Region names that must be used are:

NorthSouthEast West

-
Commission

-
The company must be able to track salesperson performance within certain regions to calculate commission.Each salesperson must be assigned only to a single region.

This commission data is currently recorded inconsistently, resulting in incorrect combinations that require manual correction. The company must have some level of automation to manage this.

Issues Issue 1

The accounting team needs an improved process for reconciling inventory to the general ledger.

Posted transactions are changing financial reporting in periods that have been closed. Unexpected changes in inventory cost for previous months are causing costing inaccuracies.The system must restrict the adjustment of costs for closed months.

The new policy will be to restrict all users to posting in the current month only, with the exception of a few employees from the accounting team.The calendar fiscal year for company must begin on June 1.

Issue 2

The accounting team uses a complex manual accrual process to determine the accounting impact of items received but not invoiced. The system must streamline the item accrual process.

Issue 3

The company often receives a higher quantity of produce items than what they order because vendors allow for spoilage or damage of produce in transit. The company does not want to allow over receipt on non-produce items.

Issue 4

The company has received comments from their auditors that invoices are not being properly compared to received inventory documents before they are posted. The company does not use warehouse management and always handlesprocesses directly from the purchase order. The company always has the following documents:

Purchase order from the procurement department receiving document from the warehouse electronicinvoice from the vendor

QUESTION 1

HOTSPOT

You need to set up a new fiscal year and restrict posting.

Which options should you use? To answer, select the appropriate options in the answer area.

NOTE: Each correct selection is worth one point.

Hot Area:

Answer Area

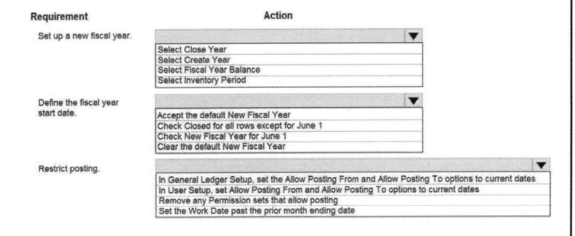

Requirement	Action
Set up a new fiscal year.	Select Close Year / Select Create Year / Select Fiscal Year Balance / Select Inventory Period
Define the fiscal year start date.	Accept the default New Fiscal Year / Check Closed for all rows except for June 1 / Check New Fiscal Year for June 1 / Clear the default New Fiscal Year
Restrict posting.	In General Ledger Setup, set the Allow Posting From and Allow Posting To options to current dates / In User Setup, set Allow Posting From and Allow Posting To options to current dates / Remove any Permission sets that allow posting / Set the Work Date past the prior month ending date

QUESTION 2

HOTSPOT

You need to configure purchase order discounting and history.

What should you do? To answer, select the appropriate options in the answer area.

NOTE: Each correct selection is worth one point.

Hot Area:

Answer Area

Requirement	Action
Configure the preset invoice level discounts.	▼ Set Discount % on Vend. Invoice Discount Set Calc. Inv. Discount to Yes Set All Discounts on Discount Posting Set Pmt. Disc. Excl. Tax to Yes
Configure the automatic invoice level discounts calculation.	▼ Set Calc. Inv. Discount to Yes on Purchase & Payables Setup Set Purch. Line Disc. Account on General Posting Setup Select Invoice Discounts on Purchase & Payables Setup Set Adjust for Payment Disc. on General Ledger Setup
Configure purchase order history.	▼ Set Archive Orders to Yes Set Archive Quotes to Always Set Copy Comments Order to Invoice to Yes Set a date for Allow Document Deletion Before

QUESTION 3
DRAG DROP

You need to configure the purchase order process to meet the auditor's requirements.

Which four actions should you perform in sequence? To answer, move the appropriate actions from the list of actions to the answer area and arrange them in the correct order.

Select and Place:

Actions	Answer Area
Run a Test Report	
Add Items, including Quantity, to the lines	
Select **Post and Invoice**	
Create a warehouse receipt	
Add a vendor	
Change the Purchase Order to a Status of **Released**	
Select **Post and Receive**	
Add a Purchaser Code	

Question Set 1

QUESTION 1

A company configures special prices for a combination of an item number and a vendor.

You need to configure optional criteria for special pricing to calculate the best price for the combination.

Which three criteria should you use? Each correct answer presents a complete solution.

NOTE: Each correct selection is worth one point.

A. Purchasing Code
B. Minimum Quantity
C. Unit of Measure Code
D. Currency Code
E. Line Discount Percentage

QUESTION 2 You are implementing Dynamics 365 Business Central for a customer who hastwo warehouses.

The customer requires the following:

   different item pricing and vendors set up for items in each warehouse   •
transactions tied to a specific location

You need to configure Business Central per the customer requirements.

Which three entities should you configure? Each correct answer presents part of the solution?

NOTE: Each correct selection is worth one point.

A. Inventory setup
B. Warehouse setup
C. Stockkeeping units
D. Item cardE. Locations

QUESTION 3 You are implementing Dynamics 365Business Central.

You use infinite items such as water, electricity, and natural gas.You need to set up the items.

Which item type should you use for infinite items?

A. Resource
B. Inventory
C. Service
D. Non-Inventory

QUESTION 4 A company uses Dynamics 365Business Central.

A customer requests that the company always use their preferred shipping provider for all sales orders.You need to configure the system to meet this requirement.

What should you do?

A. Select Shipping Advice
B. Define a shipping agent
C. Set up a Ship-to code
D. Designate a Responsibility center

QUESTION 5

You are implementing Dynamics 365 Business Central for a customer.

The customer wants to manually add many similar items.

You need to help the customer create copies of existing items.

Which three actions must be performed? Each correct answer presents part of the solution.

NOTE: Each correct selection is worth one point.

A. On the Set up Customer/Vendor/Item Templates page, create a new item template
B. Open an existing item, and then click the **Save as Template** action on the item card
C. On the Set Up Customer/Vendor/Item Templates page, edit the information in the newly created item template
D. On the Configuration Templates page, create a new template for item table
E. Create a new item, and then select the new template name to copy the information to the item

QUESTION 6
DRAG DROP

You are configuring Dynamics 365 Business Central for a company.

You need to create items.

Which item types should you use? To answer, drag the appropriate item types to the correct scenarios. Each item type may be used once, more than once, or not at all. You may need to drag the split bar between panes or scroll to view content.

NOTE: Each correct selection is worth one point.

Select and Place:

Item types

| Inventory, non-inventory, and service |
| Inventory only |
| Non-Inventory only |
| Service only |

Answer Area

Scenario	Item type
The item may be transferred between locations.	Item type
The item can be used in assembly consumption, but the quantity is not tracked.	Item type
Item will be used in sales transactions.	Item type

QUESTION 7 You are implementing Dynamics 365 BusinessCentral Online.

You receive a comprehensive price list from the customer. The customer wants you to set up the best price feature for sales by using the standard discount and pricing functionality in Business Central. You need to set up this feature.

Which three components are part of the best price calculation feature? Each correct answer presents a complete solution.

NOTE: Each correct selection is worth one point.

A. Unit cost on items
B. Sales Line Discounts
C. Discount Groups
D. Special Prices
E. Unit prices on items

Testlet 2

This is a case study. **Case studies are not timed separately. You can use as much exam time as you would like to complete each case**. However, there may be additional case studies and sections on this exam. You must manage your time to ensure that you are able to complete all questions included on this exam in the time provided.

To answer the questions included in a case study, you will need to reference information that is provided in the case study. Case studies might contain exhibits and other resources that provide more information about the scenario that isdescribed in the case study. Each question is independent of the other questions in this case study.

At the end of this case study, a review screen will appear. This screen allows you to review your answers and to make changes before you move to the next section of the exam. After you begin a new section, you cannot return to this section.

To start the case study

To display the first question in the case study, click the **Next** button. Use the buttons in the left pane to explore the content of the case study before you answer the questions. Clicking these buttons displays information such as businessrequirements, existing environment, and problem statements. When you are ready to answer a question, click the **Question** button to return to the question. **Current environment**

Cash and carry sales

When a customer makes a purchase at the company's cash and carry desk, the sale is handwritten on a three-part form.

The cash and carry associate retrieves the items listed on the order from the warehouse.
Special prices and discounts are used to move products that will expire soon or that are overstocked.Cash is accepted for payments.
The cash drawer is balanced at the end of every day. A deposit is created for the cash and given to the accountant.

Brokered sales orders

Brokered sales are called in to customer service by the brokers and sometimes directly by customers. The sales are entered into QuickBooks. Becauseinventory is not tracked in QuickBooks, the generic item **Brokered Item** is used.
Two copies of the packing slip and printed from QuickBooks and sent to the

warehouse.

Order picking

The warehouse manager provides a container and the two copies of the packing slip to a picker.Items that are out of stock are marked on both copies of the packing slip.
The shipping amount is determined and written on the packing slips.
One copy of the completed packing slip is placed in a basket for customer service. Completed orders are boxed up with a copy of the invoice and shipped to customers.

Order invoicing

Throughout the day, the customer service manager collects the packing slip copies and updates the invoices in QuickBooks.The customer service manager adds a line for shipping with the amount provided by the packer.
The customer service manager prints a copy of the final invoice and sends it to the warehouse.
The accountant uses Microsoft Word to create weekly invoices for all shipments invoiced in QuickBooks during the week for some customers.

Cash and carry sales

One-line sales invoices are saved in QuickBooks for each cash and carry sale to a miscellaneous customer.Customer details for cash and carry sales are not kept in QuickBooks. **Deposits**

The accountant receives the deposit bag from the cash and carry sales desk at the end of every day. Receipts are recorded in QuickBooks against cash and carry and brokered sales based on the deposit slips.

Brokers commission

Brokers fees are paid as a percentage of sales.
A Sales by Product/Service Summary report is run in QuickBooks every month for Brokered Item to calculate what is owned.

RequirementsCustomers

Users with permission must be able to quickly add new customers.
The original source of all customers in the accounting system must be identified to be from cash and carry or brokered sales.The company needs to keep a record of special price promotions given to specific customers.
Customers must be identified with a unique general business posting group so that the correct freight G/L account is used in sales transactions.

Sales

The customer source must be used to identify the business line, and the customer source must be indicated on every sales transactions. Customer service and cash and carry desk associates must be able to enter sales into Dynamics 365 Business Central by customer.

If a customer is not already listed in the system, a cash and carry associate or customer service associate must be able to quickly add the new customer in the process of recording the first sale.A point-of-sale system is not needed, but users must be able to record which items are purchased by customers, accept and record their payment, and print receipts indicating paid in full.

Items

The sales manager and warehouse manager must be able to set a specific timeframe for special promotion discounts on items.For special promotions, discounts must be consistent for all items in a product line using a single discount calculation.

Special pricing may be given to a retail chain or buying group. This pricing must be automatically applied when an order is taken for any of these customers. The original price must be recorded with each sale.

Customers must always be charged the lowest amount for an item at the time of the sale. For example, an overstocked olive oil has a regular price of $20 per unit. Customers in a buying group for restaurants can buy it for $18 per unit. There is an autumn promotion price for the item at $19 per unit. However, on a specific day only, there is an overstock special at a 15 percent discount off the regular price. **Sales invoices**

Warehouse workers must be able to indicate the following in the system for each order:
1. the items picked
2. the shipping charges
3. notifications, if any, that customer service needs to provide to the customer
   Items sold at a discount must show the original price, discount, and net amount on each line of the invoice. Invoices must be posted at the cash and carry desk at the time of sale. For orders, accounting must post invoices and send them tocustomers.
   Warehouse employees must be able to indicate what has been shipped on an order. They will use the G/L account for shipping charges. They need to use the correct G/L account for sales versus cost through proper assignment of salesand purchase accounts in the general posting setup.
   Some of the brokered customers require one invoice per week regardless of the number of orders or shipments. **Accounts**

   Payment terms vary by customer.
   The amount paid to brokers must be calculated from sales after invoice
   .

discounts.Broker vendors must be easily identifiable from other vendors in lists

Commission paid on sales not collected within 120 days must be deducted from brokers' next compensation payment.

Reporting

Wide World Importers requires reporting on the following:

the overall profitability of each line of business at any time for any given period

the cost of outbound shipping in the overall profitability of sales by business line in all related reportsfreight sales and cost by account in the trial balance

the cost of brokers' compensation in reporting the overall profitability of sales by business linethe effect of item discount promotions in financial statements.

Issues Pricing

Spreadsheets are used to maintain special item pricing and discounts. The only source of product line discount information is a whiteboard in the warehouse. The price charged is frequently incorrect.

Customers complain when they think they think they have not received the best price available. Promotions are sometimes applied in error after a special pricing event ends, for example, when discounts are offered temporarily to reduceoverstock.

Management cannot see original versus actual price on all sales. Discounts given by brokers requires spreadsheets and comparison between price list and price on sales invoice. Management needs to be able to quickly see the discountgiven on each sale.

Payment terms

Agreed-upon payment terms are frequently entered incorrectly on orders, causing cashflow issues.

Invoices already paid in full exist on the sales aging reports. The frequent cause of this issue is that sales from the cash and carry desk are not indicated as cash sales and are not posted as paid in full. Somebuying groups require that all invoices sent during a month be due on the 20th of the following month.

Invoicing

Paperwork is frequently misplaced between the warehouse, customer service, and accounting.

Invoices that are posted in the accounting system based on shipments and invoices that are sent to customers weekly do not match due to errors transferring the data from one document to another.Users are selecting the incorrect freight type (expense versus sales) on purchase and sales transactions, making it difficult to reconcile freight costs.

Sales placed from the cash and carry desk by customers originally acquired through a broker are not being recognized with the correct customer source. Reporting by business line is inaccurate.

Accounts

Users often forget which fields to use to enter information when they add new customers to QuickBooks. This results in errors and inconsistencies in data and affects sales reporting. Confidence in sales reporting accuracy is low.Adding new brokers is a different process than adding other purchase vendors. Users often forget which fields to select and how to correctly assign the vendor number to add new brokers.

QUESTION 1
DRAG DROP

You need to configure discounting for sales.

Which three actions should you perform in sequence? To answer, move the appropriate actions from the list of actions to the answer area.

Select and Place:

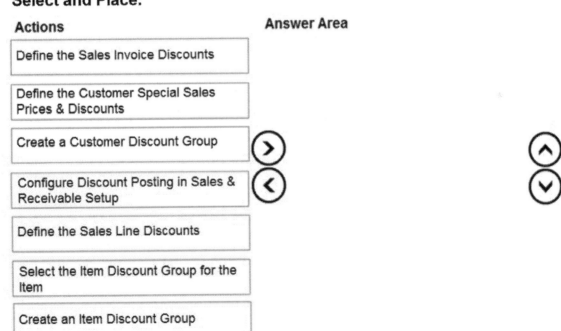

Question Set 1

QUESTION 1

DRAG DROP

You complete Payment Registration setup. The following options are enabled:

- Use this account as defaultAuto Fill Date received

You need to process a single full payment from a customer against the amounts due for two invoices by using customer payment registration.

What four actions should you perform in sequence? To answer, move the appropriate actions from the list of actions to the answer area and arrange them in the correct order.

Select and Place:

Values
Inventory
Service
Non-Inventory
Order
Lot-for-Lot
Purchase
Transfer
Assembly

Answer Area

Field	Value
Type	value
Replenishment System	value
Reordering Policy	value

QUESTION 2

You need to configure Dynamics 365 Business Central to allow for receipt of

quantities of items greater than the quantity ordered. What are two possible

ways to achieve the goal? Each correct answer presents a complete solution.

NOTE: Each correct selection is worth one point.

A. Configure a maximum order quantity for the item
B. Configure a maximum inventory level for the item
C. Set up and select an over-receipt code in the item record
D. Set up and select an over-receipt code in the vendor record

QUESTION 3
DRAG DROP

You have multiple, unpaid posted purchase invoices to reverse. Some invoices

require complete reversal while others need partial reversal. You need to

process credit memos from the posted purchase invoices.

Which actions should you perform? To answer, drag the appropriate actions to
the correct requirements. Each action may be used once, more than once, or
not at all. You may need to drag the split bar between panes or scroll to view
content.

NOTE: Each correct selection is worth one point.

Select and Place:

Actions	Answer Area	
	Requirement	**Actions**
Cancel	Automaically create and post a corrective purchase credit memo to void the initial posted purchase invoice.	Action
Correct	Enable users to manually post credit memos.	Action
Create Corrective Credit Memo	Create a new purchase invoice to replace a canceled invoice.	Action

QUESTION 4
DRAG DROP

A company uses Dynamics 365 Business Central.

The company's funds are limited and some invoices that are due cannot be paid

on time. You need to prioritize vendors when you suggest vendor payments.

Which three actions should you perform in sequence? To answer, move the appropriate actions from the list of actions to the answer area and arrange them in the correct order.

Select and Place:

Actions	Answer Area
Select **Summarize per Vendor** when you run the Suggest Vendor Payments batch job.	
Set **Vendor Priority** on the Vendor card using the lowest number, except zero, for the highest priority.	
Select **Use Vendor Priority** when you run the Suggest Vendor Payments batch job.	
Filter by Vendor Priority when you run the Suggest Vendor Payments batch job.	
Set **Vendor Priority** on the Vendor Card using the highest number for the highest priority.	
Enter **Available Amount (LCY)** when you run the Suggest Vendor Payments batch job.	

QUESTION 5

You have a Microsoft Excel file that includes journal entry data that must be

imported into Dynamics 365 Business Central. This file was previously imported

into a General Journal batch. You receive an updated version of the file that

includes corrections, deletions, and new journal entries.

Which three actions can you perform by using the Edit in Excel feature? Each
correct answer presents a complete solution.

NOTE: Each correct selection is worth one point.

A. Modify an existing line in a General Journal batch
B. Insert a new line in a General Journal batch
C. Post one or more lines in a General Journal batch
D. Request Approval for one or more lines in a General Journal batch
E. Delete an existing line from a General Journal batch

QUESTION 6 A user reports that they cannot create or view sales quotes in
Dynamics 365Business Central.

You need to help the user create and view sales quotes.

From which three cards can the user perform the required activities? Each
correct answer presents a complete solution.

NOTE: Each correct selection is worth one point.

A. Service Item
B. Opportunity
C. Job
D. Resource
E. Customer
F. Contact

QUESTION 7
DRAG DROP

You are implementing Dynamics 365 Business Central for a company.

The company must perform inventory valuation according to the following business rules:

Use the first in, first out (FIFO) costing method for all items. Include received items that are not yet invoiced on balance sheets.
Lock inventory value by closing the month.

You need to recommend a process for the company's accounting department to use.

Which three actions should you recommend be performed in sequence? To answer, move the appropriate actions from the list of actions to the answer area and arrange them in the correct order.

Select and Place:

Actions	Answer Area
Perform the Post Inventory Cost to G/L batch job	
Close the inventory period	
Include Expected Cost on the Inventory Valuation report	
Perform the Adjust Cost - Item entries batch job	
Update Standard Cost	

QUESTION 8
DRAG DROP

The accounts payable department of a company processes purchase invoices

throughout the month. A vendor sends an invoice at the end of each week that

combines all deliveries. The company wants to know how to process this

invoice.

You need to explain the steps involved in purchase invoicing.

In which order should the steps be performed? To answer, move all actions
from the list of actions to the answer area and arrange them in the correct order.

Select and Place:

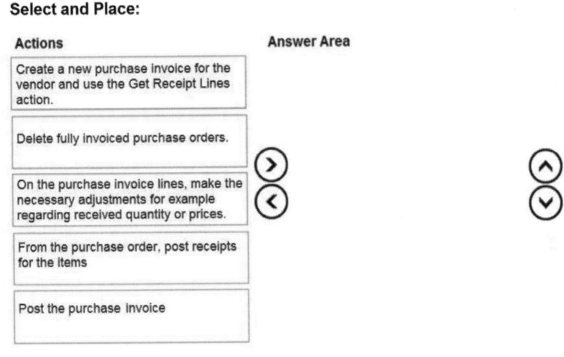

Actions

Create a new purchase invoice for the
vendor and use the Get Receipt Lines
action.

Delete fully invoiced purchase orders.

On the purchase invoice lines, make the
necessary adjustments for example
regarding received quantity or prices.

From the purchase order, post receipts
for the items

Post the purchase invoice

Answer Area

QUESTION 9
DRAG DROP

You are a functional consultant working on purchase returns in Dynamics 365 Business Central.

A customer orders 100 pieces of an item from a vendor. After receiving them into inventory and posting the invoice, the customer determines that only 50 pieces are needed.

You create a purchase return order to return 50 pieces of the item. The vendor

has authorized the return.You need to apply the return to the original purchase.

Which five actions should you perform in sequence? To answer, move the appropriate actions from the list of actions to the answer area and arrange them in the correct order.

Select and Place:

Actions	Answer Area

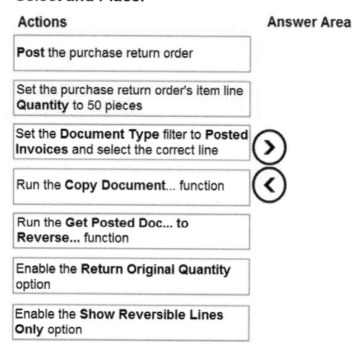

Actions

Post the purchase return order

Set the purchase return order's item line **Quantity** to 50 pieces

Set the **Document Type** filter to **Posted Invoices** and select the correct line

Run the **Copy Document...** function

Run the **Get Posted Doc... to Reverse...** function

Enable the **Return Original Quantity** option

Enable the **Show Reversible Lines Only** option

QUESTION 10

Note: This question is part of a series of questions that present the same scenario. Each question in the series contains a unique solution that might meet the stated goals. Some question sets might have more than onecorrect solution, while others might not have a correct solution.

After you answer a question in this section, you will NOT be able to return to it. As a result, these questions will not appear in the review screen.

You are implementing Dynamics 365 Business Central for a company. The

company provides subscription services to their customers. The subscription

invoices are almost identical each month.The company wants to set up

recurring sales lines for subscription invoices.

You need to create systems for creating subscription invoices.

Solution: Create a blanket order. Add the necessary lines to the blanket order.

Create the monthly sales order. Then, create the invoice.Does the solution meet

the goal?

A. Yes
B. No

QUESTION 11

Note: This question is part of a series of questions that present the same scenario. Each question in the series contains a unique solution that might meet the stated goals. Some question sets might have more than onecorrect solution, while others might not have a correct solution.

After you answer a question in this section, you will NOT be able to return to it. As a result, these questions will not appear in the review screen.

You are implementing Dynamics 365 Business Central for a company. The company provides subscription services to their customers. The subscription invoices are almost identical each month.The company wants to set up recurring sales lines for subscription invoices.

You need to create systems for creating subscription invoices.

Solution: Create a new recurring sales line. Open the relevant customers and attach the Recurring Sales Lines code to the customer. Then, run the Create Recurring Sales Invoices batch to create the invoices.Does the solution meet the goal?

A. Yes
B. No

QUESTION 12

Note: This question is part of a series of questions that present the same scenario. Each question in the series contains a unique solution that might meet the stated goals. Some question sets might have more than onecorrect solution, while others might not have a correct solution.

After you answer a question in this section, you will NOT be able to return to it. As a result, these questions will not appear in the review screen.

You are implementing Dynamics 365 Business Central for a company. The

company provides subscription services to their customers. The subscription

invoices are almost identical each month.The company wants to set up

recurring sales lines for subscription invoices.

You need to create systems for creating subscription invoices.

Solution: Create a sales quote for each customer. Add the sales lines to the

quote. Then, use the Copy Document feature to create a new invoice.Does the

solution meet the goal?

A. Yes
B. No

Testlet 2

This is a case study. **Case studies are not timed separately. You can use as much exam time as you would like to complete each case**. However, there may be additional case studies and sections on this exam. You must manage your time to ensure that you are able to complete all questions included on this exam in the time provided.

To answer the questions included in a case study, you will need to reference information that is provided in the case study. Case studies might contain exhibits and other resources that provide more information about the scenario that isdescribed in the case study. Each question is independent of the other questions in this case study.

At the end of this case study, a review screen will appear. This screen allows you to review your answers and to make changes before you move to the next section of the exam. After you begin a new section, you cannot return to this section.

To start the case study

To display the first question in the case study, click the **Next** button. Use the buttons in the left pane to explore the content of the case study before you answer the questions. Clicking these buttons displays information such as businessrequirements, existing environment, and problem statements. When you are ready to answer a question, click the **Question** button to return to the question. **Current environment**

Deliveries

   The company receives daily truckloads of products from their vendors, warehouses the products briefly, and then ships orders based on a weekly delivery cycle to each customer's store.Customers have regular standing orders that are revised and finished one week prior to delivery.
   Best for You Organics has a fleet of trucks that make deliveries according to planned routes.
   The company also has a floating route for trucks to deliver rush orders. The route is being used more often by customers and has overwhelmed the warehouse with exception processing.

Duties

The company wants to provide greater separation of duties between activities in the office and activities in the warehouse.

The accounting team enters orders for the sales team, sends pick tickers back to the warehouse, and organizes shipping documents. The accounting team invoices the orders when they receive instructions from the warehouse that an ordershipped.

Employees have expressed frustration because they need to work longer hours

to accommodate the increase in sales.The company does not use the

Advanced Warehousing function.

RequirementsSalespeople

Salespeople must be able to manage opportunities that are converted to quotes.
Salespeople must be able to release orders to the warehouse to be fulfilled once a quote is final.
Salespeople must be trained on how to determine if inventory is available

when they are completing the quote to avoid promising inventory that is not on

hand because all orders are processed one week in advance of delivery. **Team**

responsibilities

Deliveries must be shipped daily by employees in the warehouse. The office

must be responsible for completing the invoicing process.The current team

responsibilities are shown in the following graphic:

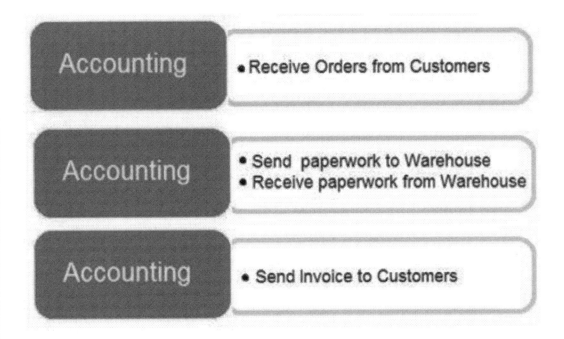

The required team responsibilities are shown in the following graphic:

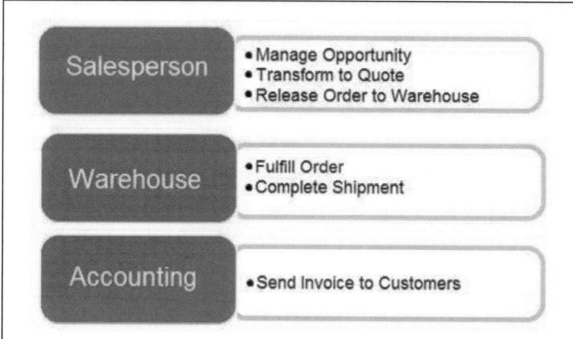

Vendor management

The company contracts with each vendor for regular discounts at the invoice level.

The company requires a pre-set discount percentage to calculate automatically when the purchaser completes a purchase order.

The company must be able to see a copy of the completed purchase order in

the system when they have new contract negotiations with their vendors.

Customerand inventory management

Sales invoices must be automatically emailed by the system to customers.
A template must be used for emails sent to customers. The template must not be altered.Customers who pre-pay their invoices must not receive a copy of their invoices.

The company warehouses all products as Case quantities. The company has difficulty recording accurate costs for product returns. The company wants to expand their capabilities for managing returns by setting up all inventory in a quantity of Each.

Reporting

The company must be able to answer two key questions when they report

financial results:Which customers are buying which items?
Which salespeople are selling in which regions?

When discussing customers, the company must refer to each Customer Group

as follows:Big Box

Franchise

Private

When discussing items, the company must refer to each Item Group as follows:

Fair Trade Free RangeGrass Fed Heirloom
Organic

Salesperson names that must be used are:

SalespersonASalespersonBSalespersonCSalespersonD

Region names that must be used are:

NorthSouthEast West

Commission

The company must be able to track salesperson performance within certain regions to calculate commission.Each salesperson must be assigned only to a single region.

This commission data is currently recorded inconsistently, resulting in incorrect combinations that require manual correction. The company must have some level of automation to manage this.

Issues Issue 1

The accounting team needs an improved process for reconciling inventory to the general ledger.

Posted transactions are changing financial reporting in periods that have been closed. Unexpected changes in inventory cost for previous months are causing costing inaccuracies.The system must restrict the adjustment of costs for closed months.

The new policy will be to restrict all users to posting in the current month only, with the exception of a few employees from the accounting team.The calendar fiscal year for company must begin on June 1.

Issue 2

The accounting team uses a complex manual accrual process to determine the accounting impact of items received but not invoiced. The system must streamline the item accrual process.

Issue 3

The company often receives a higher quantity of produce items than what they order because vendors allow for spoilage or damage of produce in transit. The company does not want to allow over receipt on non-produce items.

Issue 4

The company has received comments from their auditors that invoices are not being properly compared to received inventory documents before they are posted. The company does not use warehouse management and always handlesprocesses directly from the purchase order. The company always has the following documents:

purchase order from the procurement department receiving document from the warehouse   electronicinvoice from the vendor

QUESTION 1

You need to configure the system to meet the requirements for received items.

What should you do?

A. Set the default costing method to **Standard**

B. Turn on **Automatic Cost Posting**

C. Turn on **Expected Cost Posting**

D. Set the value of the Automatic Cost Adjustment option to **Always**

ANSWERS

Question Set 1

1. **Correct Answer:** A

   Explanation/Reference:
   Reference: https://docs.microsoft.com/en-gb/dynamics365/business-central/ui-specify-printer-selection-reports

2. **Correct Answer:** A

   Explanation/Reference:
   Reference:
   https://dankinsella.blog/add-user-in-business-central-cloud/

3. **Correct Answer:**

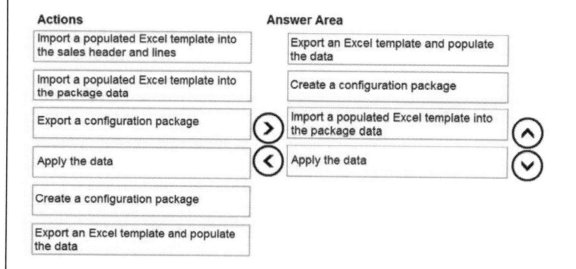

   Explanation/Reference:
   Reference: https://docs.microsoft.com/en-gb/dynamics365/business-central/admin-how-to-prepare-a-configuration-package

   https://docs.microsoft.com/en-gb/dynamics365/business-central/admin-how-to-configure-new-companies

4. **Correct Answer:**

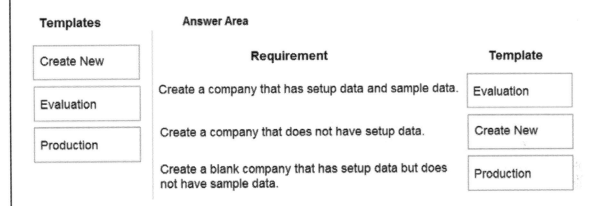

Approver limit types

| Direct approver |
| Specific approver |
| First Qualified approver |
| Approver Chain |

Answer Area

Requirement	Approver limit type
Route approval requests to the approver defined in Approval User Setup, regardless of the amount.	Direct approver
Route approval requests to the approver defined in the Workflow Response, regardless of the amount.	Specific approver
Route approval requests to a user who can approve requests for the required amount.	First Qualified approver

Explanation/Reference:
Reference: https://ebs.com.au/blog/how-approver-limit-type-works-for-purchase-order-workflows-in-microsoft-dynamics-365

5. **Correct Answer: A**

6. **Correct Answer: BD**

7. **Correct Answer:**

Templates

| Create New |
| Evaluation |
| Production |

Answer Area

Requirement	Template
Create a company that has setup data and sample data.	Evaluation
Create a company that does not have setup data.	Create New
Create a blank company that has setup data but does not have sample data.	Production

Explanation/Reference:
Reference: https://docs.microsoft.com/en-gb/dynamics365/business-central/about-new-company

Testlet 2

1   Correct Answer:

Answer Area

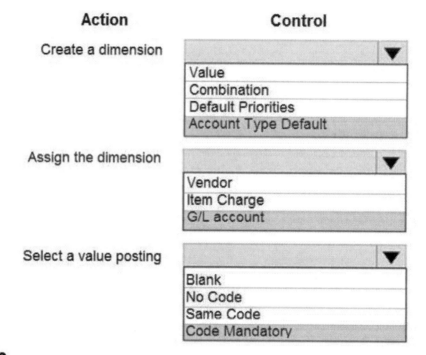

Action	Control
Create a dimension	Value / Combination / Default Priorities / **Account Type Default**
Assign the dimension	Vendor / Item Charge / **G/L account**
Select a value posting	Blank / No Code / Same Code / **Code Mandatory**

Testlet 3

1   Correct Answer:
Answer Area

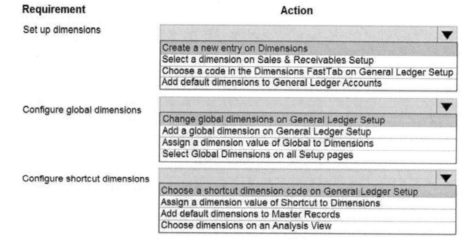

Requirement	Action
Set up dimensions	**Create a new entry on Dimensions** / Select a dimension on Sales & Receivables Setup / Choose a code in the Dimensions FastTab on General Ledger Setup / Add default dimensions to General Ledger Accounts
Configure global dimensions	**Change global dimensions on General Ledger Setup** / Add a global dimension on General Ledger Setup / Assign a dimension value of Global to Dimensions / Select Global Dimensions on all Setup pages
Configure shortcut dimensions	**Choose a shortcut dimension code on General Ledger Setup** / Assign a dimension value of Shortcut to Dimensions / Add default dimensions to Master Records / Choose dimensions on an Analysis View

Question Set 1

1   Correct Answer: D

Explanation/Reference:
Reference: https://business-central.to-increase.com/md/en-US/ui-enter-date-ranges

2   Correct Answer: C

Explanation/Reference:
Reference: https://docs.microsoft.com/en-gb/dynamics365/business-central/finance-how-to-settle-purchase-invoices-promptly

3   Correct Answer:

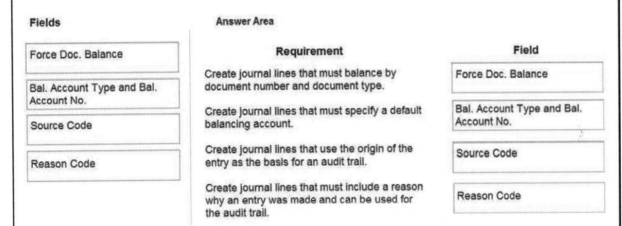

Explanation/Reference:
Reference: https://docs.microsoft.com/en-us/learn/modules/general-journal-templates-dynamics-365-business-central/1-templates

4   Correct Answer: A

Explanation/Reference:
Explanation:
The two threes in 3:3 mean a minimum of three decimal places and a maximum of 3 decimal places. In other words, it will always display three decimal places.

5   Correct Answer:

Answer Area

Control	Assignment
Bank Account Nos.	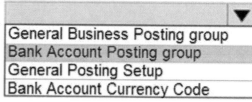
G/L Account for the bank account	

For Bank Account Nos. dropdown:
- Bank Account Posting groups
- **General Ledger Setup** *(selected)*
- Cash Flow Setup
- Source Code Setup

For G/L Account for the bank account dropdown:
- General Business Posting group
- **Bank Account Posting group** *(selected)*
- General Posting Setup
- Bank Account Currency Code

Explanation/Reference:
Reference: https://usedynamics.com/business-central/finance/general-ledger-setup/ https://docs.microsoft.com/en-gb/dynamics365/business-central/bank-how-setup-bank-accounts

6   **Correct Answer:**   A

Explanation/Reference:
Reference: https://docs.microsoft.com/en-gb/dynamics365/business-central/finance-setup-chart-accounts

7   **Correct Answer:**   C

8 Correct Answer:

Answer Area

Requirements	Action
Ensure that the costs on credit memos match the costs from the originating invoice.	▼ Select Exact Cost Reversing Mandatory Choose a No.Series for Posted Credit Memo Nos. Choose Yes to Archive Return Orders Add a Sales Credit Memo Account in General Posting Setup
Process the receipt of a return at the same time the credit memo is posted.	▼ Select Return Receipt on Credit Memo Select Shipment on Invoice Choose Skip Manual Reservation Choose Blank for Default Quantity to Ship
List a default quantity of one on the credit memo lines.	▼ Choose Yes for Default Item Quantity Choose Remainder for Default Quantity to Ship Choose No for Default Item Quantity Choose Blank for Default Quantity to Ship

9 Correct Answer:

Setups

- Bank Account Posting Groups
- Customer Posting Groups
- Inventory Posting Groups and Inventory Posting Setup
- Vendor Posting Groups
- General Posting Setup

Answer Area

Action	Setup
Automatic posting of received payment differences	Customer Posting Groups
Automatic posting to the payables account	Vendor Posting Groups
Automatic posting to different work in progress balance accounts, depending on the location	Inventory Posting Groups and Inventory Posting Setup

Explanation/Reference:
Reference: https://docs.microsoft.com/en-us/learn/modules/posting-groups-dynamics-365-business-central/1-set-up

10 Correct Answer: BDE

Explanation/Reference:
Reference: https://docs.microsoft.com/en-us/learn/modules/posting-groups-dynamics-365-business-central/4-configure

11 Correct Answer:

Answer Area

Area	Configuration
Purchase & Payables Setup	▼

Invoice Discounts for Discount Posting
Adjust for Payment Disc.
Line Discounts for Discount Posting
Calc. Inv. Discount

Area	Configuration
General Posting Setup	▼

Purch. Account
Purch. Inv. Disc. Account
Purch. Line Disc. Account
Purchase Variance Account

Explanation/Reference:

Reference:
https://docs.microsoft.com/en-gb/dynamics365/business-central/purchasing-how-record-purchase-price-discount-payment-agreements

Testlet 2

1   **Correct Answer:**   D

2   **Correct Answer:**

Answer Area

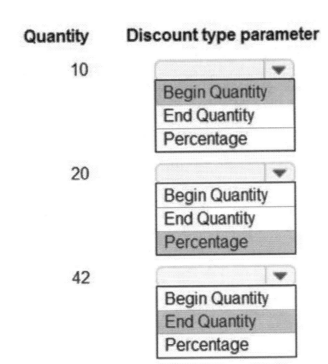

Quantity	Discount type parameter
10	Begin Quantity
20	Percentage
42	End Quantity

3 Correct Answer:

Answer Area

Configure	Control
Restrict use on	▼

General Ledger Setup
Sales & Receivable Setup
G/L Account Card
Chart of Accounts

Set value for	▼

Reconcilation account
Direct posting
Check G/L account usage
Gen.Posting Type

Testlet 3

1 Correct Answer:

Answer Area

Requirement	Action
Set up a new fiscal year.	▼

Select Close Year
Select Create Year
Select Fiscal Year Balance
Select Inventory Period

Define the fiscal year start date.	▼

Accept the default New Fiscal Year
Check Closed for all rows except for June 1
Check New Fiscal Year for June 1
Clear the default New Fiscal Year

Restrict posting.	▼

In General Ledger Setup, set the Allow Posting From and Allow Posting To options to current dates
In User Setup, set Allow Posting From and Allow Posting To options to current dates
Remove any Permission sets that allow posting
Set the Work Date past the prior month ending date

2   Correct Answer:

Answer Area

Requirement	Action
Configure the preset invoice level discounts.	▼
	Set Discount % on Vend. Invoice Discount
	Set Calc. Inv. Discount to Yes
	Set All Discounts on Discount Posting
	Set Pmt. Disc. Excl. Tax to Yes
Configure the automatic invoice level discounts calculation.	▼
	Set Calc. Inv. Discount to Yes on Purchase & Payables Setup
	Set Purch. Line Disc. Account on General Posting Setup
	Select Invoice Discounts on Purchase & Payables Setup
	Set Adjust for Paument Disc. on General Ledger Setup
Configure purchase order history.	▼
	Set Archive Orders to Yes
	Set Archive Quotes to Always
	Set Copy Comments Order to Invoice to Yes
	Set a date for Allow Document Deletion Before

3   Correct Answer:

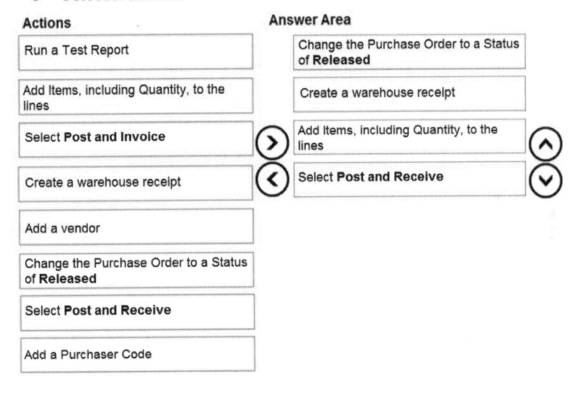

Actions

- Run a Test Report
- Add Items, including Quantity, to the lines
- Select **Post and Invoice**
- Create a warehouse receipt
- Add a vendor
- Change the Purchase Order to a Status of **Released**
- Select **Post and Receive**
- Add a Purchaser Code

Answer Area

- Change the Purchase Order to a Status of **Released**
- Create a warehouse receipt
- Add Items, including Quantity, to the lines
- Select **Post and Receive**

Question Set 1

1   Correct Answer: BCD

Explanation/Reference:
Reference: https://docs.microsoft.com/en-gb/dynamics365/business-central/purchasing-how-record-purchase-price-discount-payment-agreements

2   Correct Answer: BCD

Explanation/Reference:
Reference: https://usedynamics.com/business-central/inventory/items-using-sku/

3   Correct Answer: D

Explanation/Reference:
Reference: https://dynamicsuser.net/nav/b/peik/posts/using-infinite-components-in-a-dynamics-365-bc-production

4   Correct Answer: B

Explanation/Reference:
Reference: https://docs.microsoft.com/en-gb/dynamics365/business-central/sales-how-to-set-up-shipping-agents

5   Correct Answer: BCE

Explanation/Reference:

Reference: https://usedynamics.com/business-central/product-dev/item-templates/

6   Correct Answer:

Item types
Inventory, non-inventory, and service
Inventory only
Non-Inventory only
Service only

Answer Area

Scenario	Item type
The item may be transferred between locations.	Inventory only
The item can be used in assembly consumption, but the quantity is not tracked.	Non-Inventory only
Item will be used in sales transactions.	Inventory, non-inventory, and service

Explanation/Reference:
Reference: https://docs.microsoft.com/en-gb/dynamics365/business-central/inventory-about-item-types

7   Correct Answer: BCE
8   Explanation/Reference:
9   Reference:
10   https://docs.microsoft.com/en-gb/dynamics365/business-central/sales-how-record-sales-price-discount-payment-agreements

Testlet 2

1 Correct Answer: D

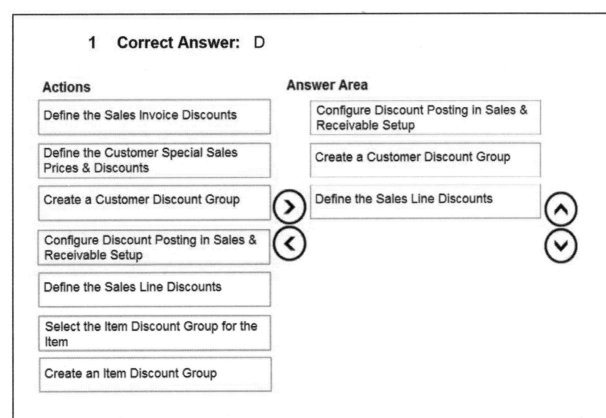

Actions

- Define the Sales Invoice Discounts
- Define the Customer Special Sales Prices & Discounts
- Create a Customer Discount Group
- Configure Discount Posting in Sales & Receivable Setup
- Define the Sales Line Discounts
- Select the Item Discount Group for the Item
- Create an Item Discount Group

Answer Area

- Configure Discount Posting in Sales & Receivable Setup
- Create a Customer Discount Group
- Define the Sales Line Discounts

Question Set 1

1 Correct Answer:

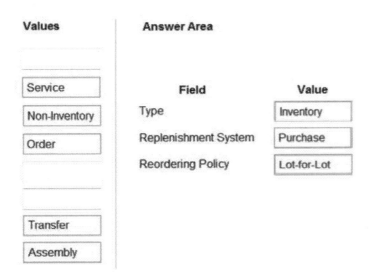

Values

- Service
- Non-Inventory
- Order
- Transfer
- Assembly

Answer Area

Field	Value
Type	Inventory
Replenishment System	Purchase
Reordering Policy	Lot-for-Lot

Explanation/Reference:

Reference: https://docs.microsoft.com/en-gb/dynamics365/business-central/receivables-how-reconcile-customer-payments-list-unpaid-sales-documents

2   Correct Answer: CD

Explanation/Reference:

Reference: https://docs.microsoft.com/en-gb/dynamics365/business-central/warehouse-how-receive-items

3   Correct Answer:

Actions

Cancel

Correct

Create Corrective Credit Memo

Answer Area

Requirement	Actions
Automaically create and post a corrective purchase credit memo to void the initial posted purchase invoice.	Correct
Enable users to manually post credit memos.	Create Corrective Credit Memo
Create a new purchase invoice to replace a canceled invoice.	Cancel

Explanation/Reference:
Reference: https://docs.microsoft.com/en-gb/dynamics365/business-central/purchasing-how-process-purchase-returns- cancellations

https://docs.microsoft.com/en-gb/dynamics365/business-central/purchasing-how-correct-cancel-unpaid-purchase- invoices

4   Correct Answer:

Actions

Select **Summarize per Vendor** when you run the Suggest Vendor Payments batch job.

Set **Vendor Priority** on the Vendor card using the lowest number, except zero, for the highest priority.

Select **Use Vendor Priority** when you run the Suggest Vendor Payments batch job.

Filter by Vendor Priority when you run the Suggest Vendor Payments batch job.

Set **Vendor Priority** on the Vendor Card using the highest number for the highest priority.

Enter **Available Amount (LCY)** when you run the Suggest Vendor Payments batch job.

Answer Area

Set **Vendor Priority** on the Vendor card using the lowest number, except zero, for the highest priority.

Enter **Available Amount (LCY)** when you run the Suggest Vendor Payments batch job.

Select **Use Vendor Priority** when you run the Suggest Vendor Payments batch job.

Explanation/Reference:

Reference: https://docs.microsoft.com/en-us/learn/modules/suggest-vendor-payments-dynamics-365-business-central/2- priority

5   Correct Answer: ABE

6   Correct Answer: BEF

7   Correct Answer:

Actions

Perform the Post Inventory Cost to G/L batch job

Close the inventory period

Include Expected Cost on the Inventory Valuation report

Perform the Adjust Cost - Item entries batch job

Update Standard Cost

Answer Area

Perform the Adjust Cost - Item entries batch job

Perform the Post Inventory Cost to G/L batch job

Close the inventory period

Explanation/Reference:

Reference: https://docs.microsoft.com/en-gb/dynamics365/business-central/finance-how-to-work-with-inventory- periods

8   Correct Answer:

Actions

Create a new purchase invoice for the vendor and use the Get Receipt Lines action.
Delete fully invoiced purchase orders.
On the purchase invoice lines, make the necessary adjustments for example regarding received quantity or prices.
From the purchase order, post receipts for the items
Post the purchase invoice

Answer Area

Create a new purchase invoice for the vendor and use the Get Receipt Lines action.
On the purchase invoice lines, make the necessary adjustments for example regarding received quantity or prices.
From the purchase order, post receipts for the items
Post the purchase invoice
Delete fully invoiced purchase orders.

Explanation/Reference:

Reference: https://docs.microsoft.com/en-gb/dynamics365/business-central/purchasing-how-to-combine-receipts

9   Correct Answer:

Actions

Post the purchase return order
Set the purchase return order's item line **Quantity** to 50 pieces
Set the **Document Type** filter to **Posted Invoices** and select the correct line
Run the **Copy Document...** function
Run the **Get Posted Doc... to Reverse...** function
Enable the **Return Original Quantity** option
Enable the **Show Reversible Lines Only** option

Answer Area

Run the **Get Posted Doc... to Reverse...** function
Enable the **Show Reversible Lines Only** option
Set the **Document Type** filter to **Posted Invoices** and select the correct line
Set the purchase return order's item line **Quantity** to 50 pieces
Post the purchase return order

Explanation/Reference:

Reference:
https://docs.microsoft.com/en-gb/dynamics365/business-central/purchasing-how-process-purchase-returns-cancellations#to-create-a-purchase-return-order-based-on-one-or-more-posted-purchase-documents

10 Correct Answer: B

Explanation/Reference:

Reference:
https://docs.microsoft.com/en-gb/dynamics365/business-central/sales-how-work-standard-lines

11 Correct Answer: A

Explanation/Reference:
Reference:
https://docs.microsoft.com/en-gb/dynamics365/business-central/sales-how-work-standard-lines

12 Correct Answer: B

Explanation/Reference:
Reference: https://docs.microsoft.com/en-gb/dynamics365/business-central/sales-how-work-standard-lines

Testlet 2

1 Correct Answer: C

Explanation/Reference:
Reference: https://docs.microsoft.com/en-gb/dynamics365/business-central/design-details-expected-cost-posting

Printed in Great Britain
by Amazon

31764995R00046